In memory of Betty Breen Burk—our mother and grandmother...
and a real mensch (1933-1970)
~ RB & AB

To Carrie - The best mensch I know.
~ AT

Intergalactic Afikoman
19419 Hwy 99
STE A, #256
Lynnwood, WA 98036
www.IntergalacticAfikoman.com

Publisher's Cataloging-In-Publication Data

Names: Burk, Rachelle, author. | Barouch, Alana, author. | Trenk, Arielle, illustrator.
Title: She's a mensch! : Jewish women who rocked the world / by Rachelle Burk and Alana Barouch ; illustrated by Arielle Trenk.
Description: Seattle : Intergalactic Afikoman, [2023] | Interest age level: 004-010. | Summary: Meet many mensches, both famous and little-known, including scientists, authors, artists, activists, athletes, and adventurers!--Publisher.
Identifiers: ISBN: 978-1-951365-11-0 | LCCN: 2022951696
Subjects: LCSH: Jewish women--Juvenile literature. | Jewish women authors--Juvenile literature. | Jewish women artists--Juvenile literature. | Jewish women athletes--Juvenile literature. | Jewish scientists--Juvenile literature. | CYAC: Jewish women. | Jewish authors. | Jewish artists. | Jewish athletes. | Jewish scientists. | BISAC: JUVENILE NONFICTION / Religion / Judaism. | JUVENILE NONFICTION / Girls & Women. | JUVENILE NONFICTION / Diversity & Multicultural.

Classification: LCC: HQ1172 .B87 2023 | DDC: 305.488924--dc23

Library of Congress Control Number: 2022951696
Printed in the USA
First Edition
2 4 6 8 10 9 7 5 3 1

She's a Mensch!

Jewish Women Who Rocked the World

by

Rachelle Burk and Alana Barouch

Illustrated by Arielle Trenk

INTERGALACTIC Afikoman

SEATTLE

They rock!

Jewish women 'round the world
have talent, strength, and smarts.
They shine like stars in every field
from science to the arts.

Jewish women through the ages have helped shape history.
These mensches are authors and activists, athletes and
adventurers, and everything in between.
Their stories inspire people everywhere.

Emma Lazarus

Emma and Miss Liberty
beckon all to shore.
One with pen and one with torch,
they greet the tired and poor.

Emma Lazarus was a poet. She cared about the plight of immigrants and fought for their rights. Emma wrote the poem engraved on the pedestal of the Statue of Liberty, which contains the powerful line, "Give me your tired, your poor, your huddled masses yearning to breathe free."

How could you welcome a stranger to your country?

Henrietta Szold

Henrietta's mission was
to help and heal the ill.
She did this with Hadassah
through tzedakah, love, and skill.

How can you
help others?

> **"Dare to dream... and when you dream, dream big."**

Henrietta Szold was the founder of Hadassah, a women's organization that helped to create hospitals and clinics in Israel. Henrietta's efforts improved healthcare for Israel's Jews and Arabs, promoting the Jewish values of "tzedakah" (charity) and "tikkun olam" (repairing the world). Thanks to her, Hadassah is now one of the largest Jewish organizations, helping people around the globe.

Marthe Cohn

Secret agent Marthe risked her life and took a chance by posing as the enemy to bring news home to France.

Q

How can you be brave?

Marthe Cohn was a French nurse who became a spy during World War II. She was able to learn the secrets of the German Army because she could speak their language and pretend to be a German nurse. Marthe won France's highest military honor for her role in helping to end the war.

FUN FACT TO MENSCH'N

Marthe was so good at keeping secrets that for 70 years she told no one she had been a spy — not even her husband and children.

Shari Lewis

Shari had a little lamb
who lived upon her hand.
The zany team delighted children
all across the land.

Shari Lewis was a famous puppeteer, ventriloquist, and singer whose television shows appeared in countries around the world. Shari performed funny skits with her puppet "Lamb Chop" for over 40 years. Shari and Lamb Chop even performed in their own Hanukkah and Passover specials.

FUN FACT TO MENSCH'N

Lamb Chop once made a speech at a meeting of the U.S. Congress, supporting better television programming for kids.
(Shari was there, too.)

Q

What funny things do you do to make people laugh?

Rena "Rusty" Kanokogi

*Rusty joined a tournament
and wore a male disguise,
then fought till judo matches welcomed
girls as well as guys.*

Rena "Rusty" Kanokogi was a judo expert. She won a championship after disguising herself as a man, since there was no women's competition. She was forced to return her medal when officials discovered that she was a woman. Rusty successfully fought to have judo added as a women's Olympic event. She is known as the Mother of Women's Judo.

How can you stand up for what you believe in?

Vera Rubin

Vera probed the galaxies
with telescopes and math.
She paved the way for girls to follow
in her cosmic path.

"Don't shoot for the stars, we already know what's there. Shoot for the space in between because that's where the real mystery lies."

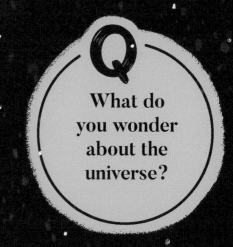

What do you wonder about the universe?

Vera Rubin was an astronomer. She studied the movement of galaxies and discovered evidence of "dark matter," material in the universe that cannot be seen. Vera encouraged women to pursue careers in astronomy and other science fields. A satellite, an asteroid, an observatory, and even an area on Mars are named after her.

Golda Meir

"Iron Lady" Golda had a vision to create a homeland for her people, which became the Jewish State.

Q

How can you be a leader?

Golda Meir was a pioneer who helped create the State of Israel. In 1969, she was elected Israel's prime minister. She is the only woman ever to serve in this position. People called her the Iron Lady because she was strong and determined.

FUN FACT TO MENSCH'N

When she immigrated to Israel as a young woman, Golda ran a chicken farm on a kibbutz.

Barbra Streisand

Barbra wows her audience
with movies, songs, and plays.
She acts! She writes! Her voice delights!
She earns abundant praise.

Barbra Streisand is a singer-songwriter, film and Broadway star, playwright, and director. She is one of the few people ever to win an Emmy, Grammy, Oscar, and Tony award. She has often played Jewish characters in movies and on stage.

Q

How can you share your talents with your family and friends?

Devra Kleiman

Devra's care and knowledge helped
endangered species thrive.
With her support, the tamarins
and pandas still survive.

FUN FACT TO MENSCH'N

In college, Devra once took a baby
dingo home to care for it. Though it
ruined her mother's basement, it led
her to her career in animal studies.

Devra Kleiman was an animal biologist. She helped to transform zoos into places to study, rescue, and protect animals—not just to display them. Her work allowed many endangered animals to be released back into the wild.

Q

How can you help animals?

Judy Blume

Judy's books are honest and they
make kids want to read,
confronting tricky troubles
in a way that children need.

**"The best books
come from someplace
deep inside."**

Judy Blume is an author of award-winning books for children and adults. Her stories, both funny and serious, have been translated into 32 languages. When people tried to ban some of her books because of their bold subjects, Judy spoke out against censorship.

Blume — the one in the middle is the green kangaroo

BLUME — DOUBLE FUDGE

Blume — Otherwise known as Sheila the Great

BLUME — THE PAIN AND THE GREAT ONE

Blume — Superfudge

BLUME — Freckle Juice

BLUME — Fudge-a-mania

Blume — Tales of a Fourth Grade Nothing

Q

What kinds of stories can you tell?

Dara Torres

Dara, the Olympic star,
could really make a splash
by racing through the water in a
record-breaking flash!

FUN FACT TO MENSCH'N

In her final Olympic Games, Dara was
so much older than her teammates that
they lovingly called her "Mom."

TORRES

Dara Torres is a swimmer who was just 17 when she competed in her first of five Olympic Games. Throughout her Olympic career, Dara won twelve medals, tying for the most won by a female swimmer. She also has the most Olympic medals of any Jewish athlete in history. Dara made multiple comebacks, and at age 41, became the oldest swimmer ever to win an Olympic medal.

Q

What activities are you great at?

Marlee Matlin

Marlee is a TV star,
and while she cannot hear,
she reads her scripts, and others' lips,
and shines in her career.

Marlee Matlin is a movie, television, and theater actor. In 1986 she received an Academy Award for best actress, making her the first deaf person to win an Oscar. She gave her acceptance speech in sign language. Growing up, Marlee attended a synagogue for the deaf with her family, where she celebrated her bat mitzvah.

"Silence is the last thing the world will ever hear from me."

Q

How many different ways can you communicate with others?

Ruth Bader Ginsburg

Ruth was feisty, fair, and wise,
and made sure laws were just.
A champion of equality,
she had the nation's trust.

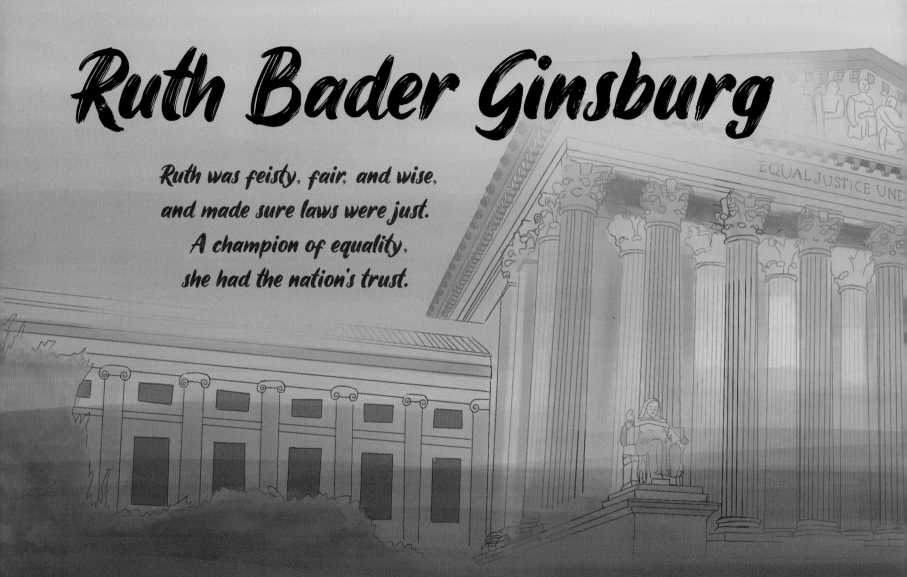

Ruth Bader Ginsburg was a U.S. Supreme Court Justice, a position she held for 27 years. She was the second woman and the first Jewish woman on the Supreme Court. Throughout her career, Ruth fought for women's rights, and for everyone to be treated equally regardless of their race, religion, or gender.

"Women belong in all the places where decisions are being made."

Q

How can you solve disagreements in ways that are fair?

Nalini Nadkarni

*Nalini finds a hidden world
each time she climbs a tree.
She studies precious life within
the forest canopy.*

Nalini Nadkarni is a scientist who explores plant and
animal life in the treetops of rain forests. She works
with artists, dancers, and musicians to creatively raise
awareness about the importance of trees. Nalini shares her
knowledge in schools, places of worship, and even prisons,
encouraging people to understand and protect trees.

Q

What hidden worlds would you like to explore?

FUN FACT TO MENSCH'N

Nalini assisted *National Geographic* and the Mattel toy company in creating a new line of scientist Barbies. To say thank you, Mattel gave Nalini a one-of-a-kind Barbie that looks like her.

Judit Polgár

With passion, practice, perseverance,
Judit found success.
She knocked out knights and conquered kings...
Long live the Queen of Chess!

Judit Polgár is a world champion chess player from Hungary. She beat adult chess masters when she was still a child. After a world champion said that women shouldn't play chess, Judit responded by defeating him. By age 12 she became the top-ranked female chess player in the world, and she remains the greatest female chess player of all time.

"Make good moves in life. Set your goals high and reach the impossible."

Q How can you get better at something you love?

Cheryl and Nikki Bart

*Cheryl hiked with Nikki
as a mother-daughter team.
They scaled the Seven Summits,
living life to the extreme.*

Cheryl Bart and her daughter **Nikki** are
Australian mountaineers. Together they climbed
the highest mountain on each of the seven
continents. They began their daring quest when
Nikki was only 16 years old. While on Mount Everest,
they celebrated the Passover holiday with a seder.

Q

What great adventures do you dream of going on?

"Abraham and Moses may have been the first Jewish mountaineers. But they weren't the last." ~ Cheryl

Annie Leibovitz

*Annie's pictures are among
the greatest ever seen.
Her photos capture singers, actors,
athletes, and a queen!*

Annie Leibovitz is a world-renowned photographer. Her pictures have been seen on magazine covers and in museums around the world. She has photographed famous people including Barack and Michelle Obama, Queen Elizabeth, rock legends, and movie stars.

Q

What would you like to take pictures of?

FUN FACT TO MENSCH'N

As a college student, photos Annie took while living on a kibbutz in Israel helped her land her first big job at *Rolling Stone* magazine.

April N. Baskin

April leads her fellow Jews
to joyfully embrace
diversity in heritage,
identity, and race.

"Diversity is the reality and future of Jewish life."

April N. Baskin is the founder of Joyous Justice, an organization that works toward equality, understanding, and well-being among people of different races and cultures. She also helps the Jewish community learn how to better welcome Jews of diverse backgrounds. April strives to create a world full of joy where no one is left out.

Q
How can you make sure that no one feels left out?
DO JUSTICE LOVE MERCY

Jessica Meir

For Jessica, the sky's the limit
in her bold career.
Beneath the sea or to the stars,
she seeks a new frontier.

Jessica Meir is an astronaut and scientist. Before she joined the NASA Space Corps, she was an aquanaut in an undersea research mission. In 2019, she was part of the first all-woman spacewalk.

Q

What can you learn from exploring new places?

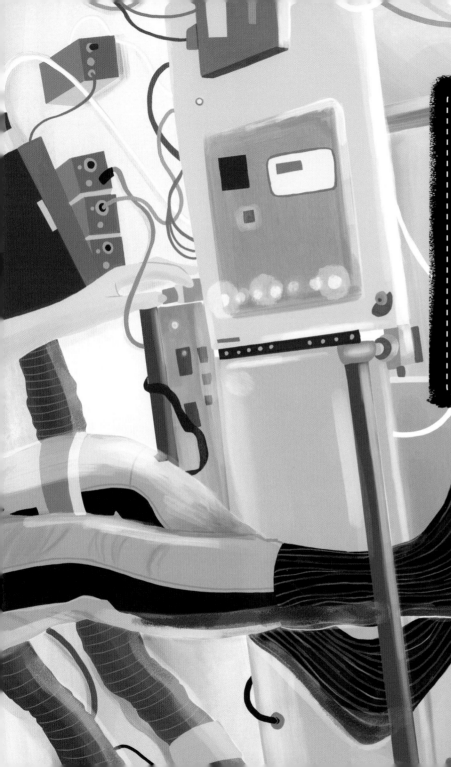

FUN FACT TO MENSCH'N

"Astro Jessica" celebrated Hanukkah in space by wearing festive holiday socks and sending a Happy Hanukkah message to Earth on social media.

She's in a lab, or out in space,
or on the judge's bench.
That Jewish woman, brave and bright,
you know her...

she's a mensch!

Q

How will

YOU

be a mensch?

Timeline

1883
EMMA LAZARUS writes her poem, *The New Colossus*

1912
HENRIETTA SZOLD founds Hadassah

1945
MARTHE COHN spies for the French during World War II

1988
RUSTY KANOKOGI brings women's judo to Olympics

1986
MARLEE MATLIN makes history as first deaf actor to win an Academy Award

1983
BARBRA STREISAND directs and stars in *Yentl*

1991
JUDIT POLGÁR becomes chess grandmaster at age 15

1993
RUTH BADER GINSBURG is appointed to U.S. Supreme Court

2008
CHERYL & NIKKI BART climb Mt. Everest

2008
DARA TORRES wins medals in her fifth Olympic Games

1956
SHARI LEWIS introduces her puppet Lamb Chop to TV audiences for the first time

1969
GOLDA MEIR is elected prime minister of Israel

1970s
VERA RUBIN provides proof of dark matter

1981
NALINI NADKARNI performs first survey of rain forest treetops

1980
JUDY BLUME publishes her popular children's book *Superfudge*

1978
DEVRA KLEIMAN leads research department at the National Zoo

2009
ANNIE LEIBOVITZ photographs the Obama family

2019
APRIL N. BASKIN founds Joyous Justice

2019
JESSICA MEIR takes part in the first all-woman spacewalk

18 Honorable Menschen

Menschen is the Yiddish plural of mensch!

Aly Raisman	Olympic gymnast who performed her gold medal-winning floor routine to Hava Nagila
Elena Kagan	Supreme Court Justice
Beverly Sills	"America's Queen of Opera"
Virginia Morris Pollak	Artist who used clay to create healing devices for wounded soldiers during World War II
Maya Plisetskaya	Russian prima ballerina, one of the greatest of the 20th century
Diane Von Furstenberg	World-famous fashion designer and philanthropist
Emmy Noether	Mathematician who Einstein called a genius
Gertrude B. Elion	Nobel Prize-winning scientist who developed life-saving medicines
Angela Buchdahl	First woman to serve as both rabbi and cantor, and the first Asian-American ordained as a rabbi
Susan Wojcicki	Longtime CEO of Youtube, and involved in many social justice causes

Maya Plisetskaya

Tomer Margalit

Clara Lemlich

PICKET
LADIES TAILORS
STRIKERS

Aly Raisman

Angela Buchdahl

Blair Braverman

Clara Raven	One of the first female doctors to serve in World War II
Blair Braverman	Dogsledder who completed the Iditarod, Alaska's famous dogsled race
Rosalind Franklin	First scientist to observe and record the structure of DNA, life's building block
Carole King	One of the most successful singer-songwriters of all time
Gal Gadot	Israeli actor known for her starring role as the superhero "Wonder Woman"
Tomer Margalit	World champion dancer from Israel who danced a Wonder Woman routine in her wheelchair. Inspired by the performance, **Gal Gadot** called Tomer the "true superhero"
Naomi Wadler	Young social justice activist. Organized a school protest and spoke at a major rally to end gun violence when she was just 11
Clara Lemlich	Union activist from Ukraine. Led factory strikes in New York, resulting in safer conditions and better pay for workers

Naomi Wadler

Diane Von Furstenberg

What is a mensch?

To be called a mensch is perhaps the ultimate Jewish compliment. *Mensch* is a Yiddish word for someone who is truly good—a person of integrity and honor. "What a mensch!" one might say after seeing someone act in a kind and generous way.

Many people assume that the word mensch can only be used to describe a man, but men, women, and children can all be mensches!

This book highlights a few inspiring and exciting Jewish women, but many more pages could have been filled by such mensches. Be on the lookout—there are mensches everywhere!

Mother-daughter team **RACHELLE BURK** and **ALANA BAROUCH** wrote this book as a "pandemic project," working together over video chat. They team up on other adventures as well, such as scuba diving and hiking with their family. They also volunteered together for years on their local first aid squad.

RACHELLE writes fiction and nonfiction books for children. She also entertains kids as Mother Goof Storyteller and Tickles the Clown. Rachelle is a retired social worker who enjoys traveling and making mosaic art.

Visit Rachelle at www.rachelleburk.com.

ALANA is a registered nurse specializing as a clinical organ donation coordinator. Alana enjoys travel, rock climbing, acrobatics, and singing. This is her first book.

ARIELLE TRENK is a jack-of-all-trades illustrator with a passion for storytelling. Her projects have included painting pianos displayed on the streets of New York, illustrating presidential candidates for a media outlet, editorials for alumni magazines, and more. You can find her illustrations on her website, www.arielletrenk.com.